SNIFF-SNUFF-SNAP!

Lynley Dodd

Gareth Stevens Publishing
A WORLD ALMANAC EDUCATION GROUP COMPANY

The sun was hot,
the day was still,
the animals came
to drink their fill.
Down past rocks
and thornbush tree,
down to the waterhole,
one
two
three.

3

One bossy warthog,
tail up high,

Two yellow weaver birds,
passing by.
"EEEEEEEE!"
squealed the warthog,
"SNIFF-SNUFF-SNAP!"
He chased them away ...
BUT

they both
sneaked
back.
Back to the waterhole,
green and brown
and slowly,
the water went down
and
down.

Three shy dik-diks,
tip-tap-toe,
four old baboons
in a grumpy row.
"EEEEEEEE!"
squealed the warthog,
"SNIFF-SNUFF-SNAP!"

He chased them away ...
BUT

they all
sneaked
back.
Back to the waterhole,
green and brown
and slowly,
the water went down
and
down.

Five fine leopards,
out of sight,
six striped zebras,
black and white.
"EEEEEEEE!"
squealed the warthog,
"SNIFF-SNUFF-SNAP!"

He chased them away ...
BUT

they all
sneaked
back.
Back to the waterhole,
green and brown
and slowly,
the water went down
and
down.

Seven tall giraffes
with feet astride,
eight fat elephants,
side by side.
"EEEEEEEE!"
squealed the warthog,
"SNIFF-SNUFF-SNAP!"

He chased them away ...
BUT

they all
sneaked
back.
Back to the waterhole,
green and brown
and slowly,
the water went down
and
down.

Back came the warthog,
tired and hot,
for a long,
cool drink
at his favorite spot.
Down past rocks
and thornbush tree,
he came to the waterhole
BUT
what did he see?

THICK

BROWN

MUD

For a free color catalog describing Gareth Stevens' list of high-quality books and multimedia programs, call 1-800-542-2595 (USA) or 1-800-461-9120 (Canada). Gareth Stevens Publishing's Fax: (414) 225-0377.

Other GOLD STAR FIRST READER Millennium Editions:

and also by Lynley Dodd:

A Dragon in a Wagon
Hairy Maclary from Donaldson's Dairy
Hairy Maclary Scattercat
Hairy Maclary and Zachary Quack
Hairy Maclary's Caterwaul Caper
Hairy Maclary's Rumpus at the Vet
The Smallest Turtle

Hairy Maclary, Sit
Hairy Maclary's Showbusiness
The Minister's Cat ABC
Schnitzel von Krumm Forget-Me-Not
Slinky Malinki Catflaps

Library of Congress Cataloging-in-Publication Data available upon request from publisher. Fax (414) 225-0377 for the attention of the Publishing Records Department.

ISBN 0-8368-2677-9

This edition first published in 2000 by
Gareth Stevens Publishing
A World Almanac Education Group Company
1555 North RiverCenter Drive, Suite 201
Milwaukee, WI 53212 USA

First published in 1995 in New Zealand by Mallinson Rendel Publishers Ltd. Original © 1995 by Lynley Dodd.

Printed in the United States of America

1 2 3 4 5 6 7 8 9 04 03 02 01 00